New Beginnings

New Beginnings

EUGENE RISI

Copyright © 2023 Eugene Risi.

All rights reserved. No part of this publication may be reproduced, distributed, or transmitted in any form or by any electronic or mechanical means, including information storage and retrieval systems, without a prior written permission from the publisher, except by reviewers, who may quote brief passages in a review, and certain other noncommercial uses permitted by the copyright law.

Library of Congress Control Number: 2023902489

ISBN: 978-1-960113-87-0   (PB)
ISBN: 978-1-960113-88-7   (HB)
ISBN: 978-1-960113-86-3   (E-book)

Book Ordering Information

The Regency Publishers, International
7 Bell Yard London W02A2JR

info@theregencypublishers.com
info@theregencypublishers.com
+44 20 8133 0466

Printed in the United States of America

Dedicated to all those who share my yearning
for a New Beginning……

TABLE OF CONTENTS

Acknowledgements ix

Preface xi

New Beginnings 1

Seeds Of Awakening 17

Too Busy 37

ACKNOWLEDGEMENTS

No publication is the work of one person alone.

I'd like to thank my sister, Mary, and my niece, Nicola, for their patient proof-reading of the poems and their invaluable suggestions.

And my other sister, Paula, and my nephew Laurence, for their help with the photo selection.

Thanks is also owing to Daphne and Janine, my agents at Breakthrough (now Regency) Publishers for their patient assistance and forthright advice and of course to all the people working behind the scenes with them to produce this inspiring volume.

Finally, I'd like to thank all those who read the poems in this anthology. May you be inspired by them!

PREFACE

'The difference between poetry and verse, then, is the difference between an explorer and a tour guide. Verse tells us, finally, that all is well. Poetry, on the contrary, tells us that things are not as we thought they were. Verse does not ask us to change our lives.'

It seems incontrovertible that we are living in a time of great crisis in which things that seemed stable only a few years back are now in question. The word crisis itself, however, points in two directions. The one is in the direction of chaos and destruction. This leads to fear, perhaps even anger at the sense of impotence it generates. The other sense of crisis is opportunity, as the breakdown of the old can also bring a new sense of possibility and renovation. It conjures the image of the phoenix rising from the ashes of its own self-destruction. This presupposes a faith in the cyclical nature of experience, something we witness yearly in the seasons but also in the cycles of birth and death in our own lives: childhood dies into adolescence and adulthood, youth into old age, each with its special quality and even danger. The poetry in this anthology honours this cyclical nature of existence, so often at odds with the linear sense of time which governs our lives from birth to death here in the West and indeed all modern societies. I have a feeling that the limitation inherent in this linear and non-cyclical view of life is part of the deeper crisis of this particular moment in history and of our civilisation itself. This linearity underpins all our economic and political endeavours in our pursuit of ever more profit and power, even though it has become apparent that the earth as an ecological unit can no longer support either. We have reached the limits of an unsustainable way of life but find ourselves unable to let it go or even conceive of an alternative.

These poems are my own humble attempt to point a way. Why poetry?

Because poetry by its nature (I am not here referring to verse) eschews the linearity of prose, so essential to our practical endeavours, but inadequate to engage the other aspects of human experience. To express this more simply, while prose engages the head, poetry engages both heart and head together. The medium is one with the message. If we wish to grasp the extraordinary opportunities of the present crisis, we need to embrace the deeper truths about ourselves as imaginative and spiritual beings and poetry can help us to do this as it engages us imaginatively and emotionally. My own experience of great poetry has been that movement of inspiration, that moment of apprehension that leaves me in awe at new possibility or in wonder at entrenched but unnoticed beauty. It is ineffable and beyond words although words have been used to create it. (My own poems include homage to some of my finest inspiration.) It is my hope that the poems in this anthology can do something similar. The photographs accompanying the poetry are there to aid the process but I hope that you will allow the text itself to transport you to a new experience of who you are and what we can all be together if only we embrace that (deeper, poetic, non linear) vision.

NEW BEGINNINGS

I

Spring
is like the lymph
in a young tree
wood
supple
        still green
pushing upward
        ever upward
into leaf and flower

Eden -
our springtime -
was that lymph
our life-force
pushing upward
ever upward
into lush abundance

II

But
now
our trees are husks
in the desert of our frozen winters
brittle dry sapless branches reaching upward
in barren salute

the fruitlessness
of strangled promise

Only the roots
our deepest roots
maintain the memory of sap-filled summers
and long for peace to spring

III

Why have our minds grown
rankling thorns
smothering
the seed
containing
within
the memory of Eden?

The whisperings of serpents
taunt us with promises of divinity
Heaven spurned
Oneness is shattered
I versus I
beholds Itself
in a cracked mirror
Projected shards of jagged consciousness
rend the veil of consciousness
We are suddenly afraid of ourselves

Nature's abundance now scarce
covetousness
       and self-aggrandisement
cover our nakedness
dominion our new song of survival

Our world
born in an act of violence
has undone the promise of peace
but not broken its longing

The tree of life
undone
alone
stands
witness
to other music.

IV

Deep winter is unleashed
a desolate landscape of white ice and bitter snow
A wasteland of our own making
    forged out of acts
        of greed and tribal vindication

The ruthless Snow Queen
Goddess of Capital
holds her sway
Like a medieval potentate she counts her gold
while her minions feast
The hungry landscape a charnel house of mangled bones
Trenches and battlefields strewn with the blood offering of our young

V

Call them what we will
Then 'heretics' or 'blasphemers', now 'savages' or 'terrorists'
the tactic of naming and blaming
is a tool of dominion
history's fool belying theft and murder
Jezebel's land grab of Naboth's vineyard
foreshadows pandas rolling into Poland
(to name but one)
Sophistication in itself cannot guarantee peace
only more sophisticated war
The seeds of Auschwitz lie in Cain's slaughter of Abel
the acrid smoke of burnt offerings curling offensively to heaven

VI

Our gods
laugh at us
Demons crazed by the smell of blood
licking their chops
We are puppets in their hands
until we renounce this caricature of ourselves
and cutting the strings
seek instead
the sap
within

VII

Drop your sword
and walk barefoot on the grass of peace
Feel its cool dew
and prickling caress
Hear again the winds of
brother- and sisterhood
ruffling tousled hair
See again the light in eyes
which have forgotten to shield their broken enmity
and
which
breaking forth
enlighten and embrace
Participate again in commensality
salt sprinkled on renewed friendship
forgiveness the oil of condiment

VIII

Come storms of spring!
Let the returning sun and gentle rain
pierce this frozen mantle
and relinquish its gasping
                               grasping grip

Compassion un-locked within
first flickering
now bursting
         into flame
melting snow and ice
hearts of stone
again grateful
God's earth's abundance
evenly shared

IX

Masters and Poets have spoken
the clarion call to peace is sounded
and reverberates
like a thunder clap around the globe

This poem is the harbinger
of new beginnings
a new shoot
delicately cradled by the warm earth

Hear it
and breathe its promise into being

X

Eden - recovered - is an act
of peace and sharing
of honouring and being honoured
love clothing all
earth's childhood
remembered
Eden's banishment
undone

The angel guarding the gate
barring our way
revokes her silent sword
war renounced
swords beaten into ploughshares
we stand
readmitted

Embattled
minds
embrace

Love is within
pushing upward
ever upward
bunged up juices
strangled joy

Spring of peace!

SEEDS OF AWAKENING

The Songs Of The Master

dedicated to the Masters past and present
who have graced our planet

I

My birth is shrouded in mystery and so will be my death
But then so is yours
You are not who you think you are
You are not place
or time
Born in the forgotten mists of eternity
You stretch endless
in the infinite reaches
 of non-time and non-space
This life is a point on a page of infinite dimension
Its beginning is its end
a pinprick of consciousness
out of eternity
Our coming is our going
mine and yours
I know this
It is my desire that you know it too
My forgetting is your remembering
My birth your death
My dying your rebirth

II

The song of the ancient one is woven in colours
you have forgotten
It is the song of the universe
you cannot see
How to describe the infinite in words
How to paint the colours of no-time no-place
in the colours of time and place
the memory of eternity
remains
like a bubble of light
deep within
pushing upward
ever upward
and exploding into air
at the surface

III

Where must I begin to remind you who you are
You are so involved in the business of busy-ness
so entwined in the coils of who you are not
Like a spider caught in webs of its own making
Come with me
and see who you are
Come with me
and look again at what you have forgotten
All you need to do is to stop spinning the threads of forgetting

IV

You either have peace or war
You cannot have both
Choose again
You either have love or hate
All the sophistry in the world cannot change this
Choose again
You either have scarcity or plenty
All of you
Your plenty cannot be the other's hunger and thirst
Choose again
You either embrace the earth or kill it
Your war against Nature is a war against yourselves
Choose again

V

Embattled minds cannot grasp stillness
Thoughts spun in violence beget violence
The rhetoric of peace spawns
Swirling mazes, whirls of words in contradiction
Falsifying meaning

Point scoring is lawyers' fare
Negotiation masquerading as peace

My kingdom is not of this word

VI

Your thoughts are founded in violence
If you want roses
Plant peace
If you want lotus blossoms
Sow seeds of awakening

VII

Your mind is unable to grasp the reality of the enlightened ones
How can the finite fathom the infinite
How can violence fathom non-violence

VIII

First there is the seed then the plant
My coming is the seed of your return

IX

Do not hold onto my form
Before I was
I am

X

Your theology is the form pointing to the formless
It cannot contain it
It speaks to mind
But cannot transcend it
Idolatry is not limited to statues or pictures
The images you grasp at can be words spun into a web of delicate
but deadly silk
Gossamer threads
En-closing your mind
Suffocating spirit
attitudes of premature righteousness
stronger than the links of any chain
Do not seek me in images
I am ineffable
Do not seek me in words
They are finite
Seek me within yourself
Only the infinite can grasp
the infinite

XI

Every age proclaims me
Churches, Temples, Mosques
Brick and mortar
silver and gold
Erected to honour the hour of my coming
My fluidity
solidified

Every age sings songs to me
Words in languages themselves monuments
to my passing
there
among you
Water in a river
its eternal now damned at a moment of its flowing

Every age bows before the image of me as I was
Images bejewelled and polished gold
A mirror of its own desires
magnified into godhead

Every age
proclaims
its revelation final
Its Buddha, Christ or Prophet
definitive
Are you so small you must erect your superiority on my shoulders
Must I be the excuse for your inquisitions and your wars

Could eternity be born but once
Behoven to the meanness of time
Could the everpresent abandon Itself
Love confined to one caress
in the folds of eternity

XII

Hold not onto
an image of me
frozen in time
It is the tomb of spirit
denying present recognition
I will not
cannot
be buried with you

Our present encounter
contains a spark of recognition
That leap into eternity
that liberates within you
the eternal trying to be born
Look at me
as I call your name

I am the lighted one
The whisper of eternity
the eternal word

I AM

TOO BUSY

Are you too busy?

Too busy dwelling on the past
or thinking about your problems
or planning for the future?
Too busy running the home
or managing the children
or your business?
Too busy to take time to look around and see
the people around you,
and smile
or say hello
or give a helping hand
and remember to whisper a prayer of blessing or
gratitude within your heart?
Too busy to stop to feel the sun on your face
or the first drops of hot rain in a summer drought?
Too busy to scrunch through the red riot of autumn leaves
or run open-mouthed to catch and taste the flakes of falling snow?
Too busy to marvel at the first sign of spring
and feel the warming earth underfoot?
Too busy to scour the blueness of the sky
or listen to the wind and feel it to sweep you up in its playful embrace?
Too busy to do something just for the hell of it
like you did as a child
and not count what you might get out of it?

Too busy to drop a coin in the begging bowl
without scowling about how hard you work
or lecturing the beggar in your mind about what he will spend it on?
Too busy to forget to talk and taking a hand in yours just walk
heart in heart?
Too busy to make love in the dead of night not with your body only
but with your soul?
Too busy to take time out of your busy schedule
and just for a moment be?
Too busy to marvel at all things 'counter, original, spare, strange'
and seeing beyond the many
apprehend the One?
Too busy, even in moments of busyness, to remain present in and to all?
Too busy to listen to that small inner voice become a raging waterfall
and looking into the light of the sun
touch the face of God?

www.ingramcontent.com/pod-product-compliance
Lightning Source LLC
LaVergne TN
LVHW050138080526
838202LV00061B/6522